MAMMA MIA!
EASY PIANO

MAMMA MIA!

D1420090

WISE PUBLICATIONS
PART OF THE MUSIC SALES GROUP
LONDON / NEW YORK / PARIS / SYDNEY / COPENHAGEN / BERLIN / MADRID / TOKYO

PUBLISHED BY
WISE PUBLICATIONS
8/9 FRITH STREET,
LONDON W1D 3JB, UK

EXCLUSIVE DISTRIBUTORS:
MUSIC SALES LIMITED
DISTRIBUTION CENTRE, NEWMARKET ROAD,
BURY ST EDMUNDS, SUFFOLK IP33 3YB, UK
MUSIC SALES PTY LIMITED
120 ROTHSCHILD AVENUE, ROSEBERY, NSW 2018, AUSTRALIA.

ORDER NO.AM984995
ISBN 1-84609-447-X
THIS BOOK © COPYRIGHT 2006 WISE PUBLICATIONS,
A DIVISION OF MUSIC SALES LIMITED

COVER LOGO TYPE BY COURTESY OF McCABES
PHOTOS BY COURTESY OF PETER THOMPSON ASSOCIATES
PRINTED IN THE EU

www.**musicroom**.com

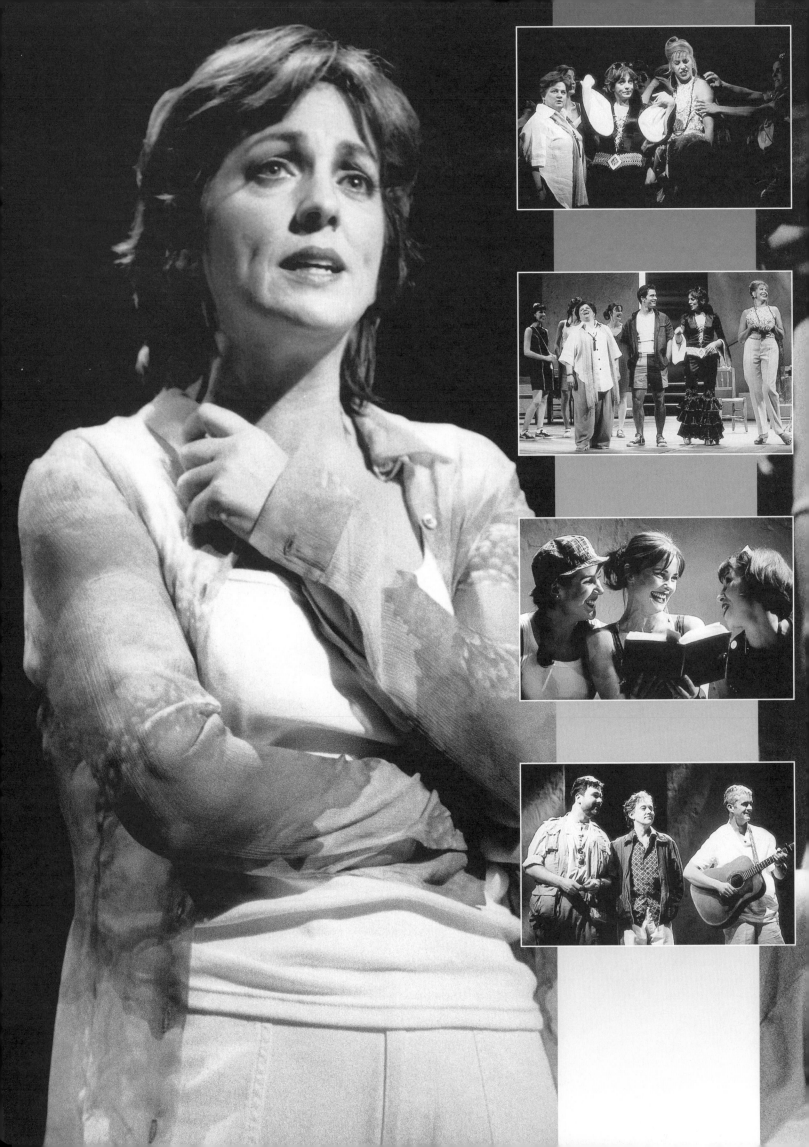

Gimme! Gimme! Gimme!
(A Man After Midnight)

Words & Music by Benny Andersson & Bjorn Ulvaeus

Chiquitita

Words & Music by Benny Andersson & Bjorn Ulvaeus

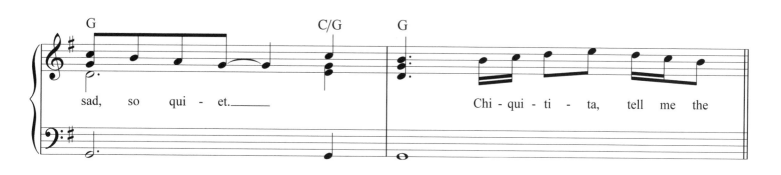

sad, so qui - et.____

Chi - qui - ti - ta, tell me the

♩ = 86 a tempo

truth.

I'm a shoul - der

you can cry on,____

your_____ best friend, I'm the one you

must re - ly on._____

You were al - ways sure of your - self.

Now I see you've

bro - ken a fea - ther.____

13

Dancing Queen

Words & Music by Benny Andersson, Bjorn Ulvaeus & Stig Anderson

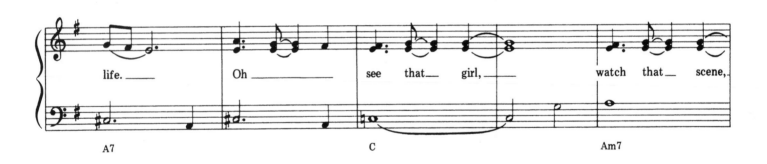

C   G   C

Fri - day night and the lights are low,

G   Em   D

look - ing out for a place to go. Oh when they play the right

G   D   G   D   Em

mu - sic, get - ting in the swing, You come to look for a king.

D   Em   C

1. A - ny - bod - y could be that guy;
2. You're a tea - ser, you turn 'em on,

G   Em

night is young and the mu - sic's high.
leave 'em burn - ing and then you're gone.

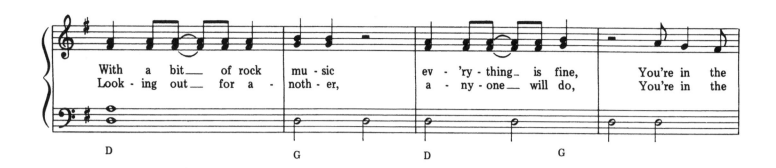

With a bit___ of rock mu - sic ev - 'ry - thing__ is fine, You're in the
Look - ing out___ for a - noth - er, a - ny - one__ will do, You're in the

D   G   D   G

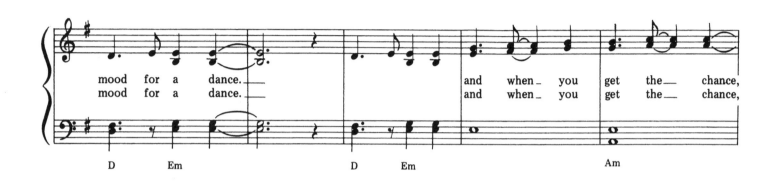

mood for a dance.___ and when__ you get the__ chance,
mood for a dance.___ and when__ you get the__ chance,

D   Em   D   Em   Am

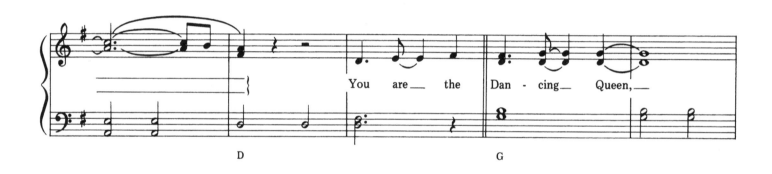

You are__ the Dan - cing__ Queen,___

D   G

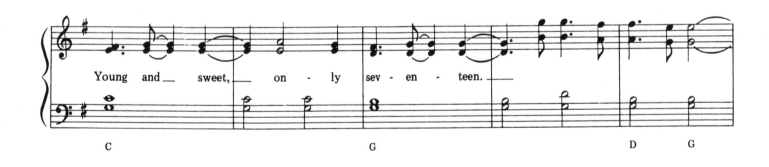

Young and__ sweet,___ on - ly sev - en - teen.___

C   G   D   G

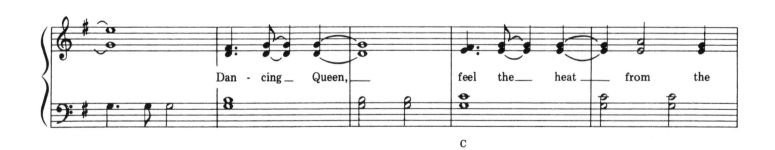

Dan - cing__ Queen,___ feel the__ heat___ from the

C

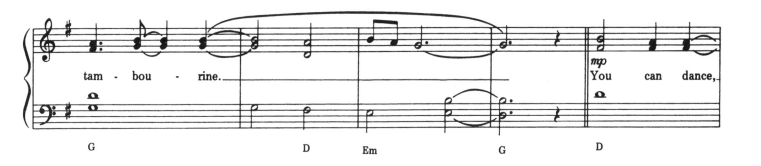

tam - bou - rine. ___ You can dance,

G   D   Em   G   D

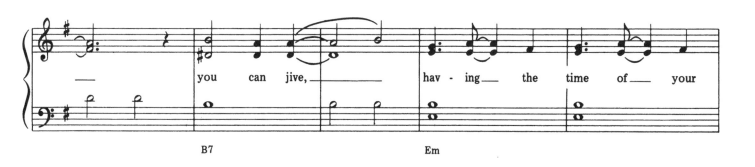

___ you can jive, ___ hav - ing ___ the time of ___ your

B7   Em

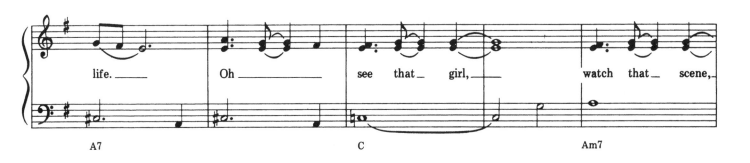

life. ___ Oh ___ see that ___ girl, ___ watch that ___ scene,

A7   C   Am7

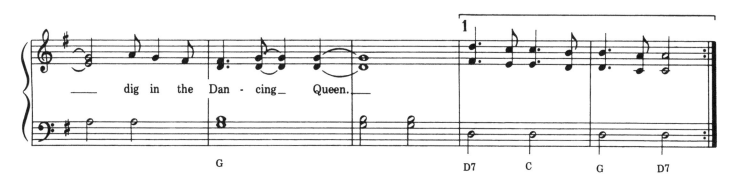

___ dig in the Dan - cing ___ Queen. ___

G   D7   C   G   D7

Repeat and Fade

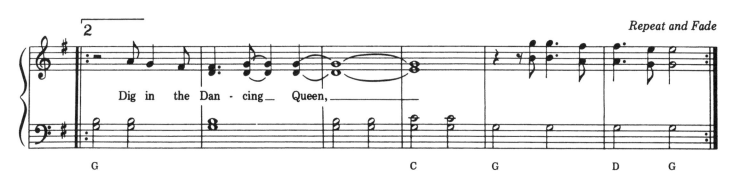

Dig in the Dan - cing ___ Queen, ___

G   C   G   D   G

Does Your Mother Know

Words & Music by Benny Andersson & Bjorn Ulvaeus

1. Your so hot,___ teas - ing me.___ So you're blue,___
2. I can see___ what you want.___ But you seem

___ but I can't take a chance on a kid like you.___
___ pret - ty young to be search - ing for that kind of fun.___

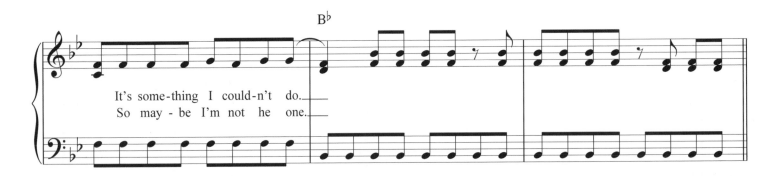

It's some-thing I could-n't do.___
So may - be I'm not he one.

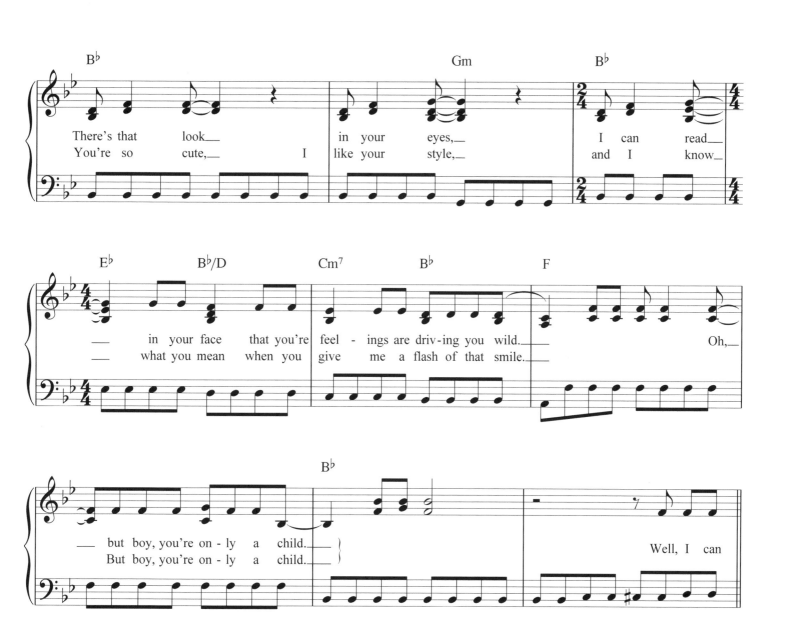

Honey Honey

Words & Music by Benny Andersson, Bjorn Ulvaeus & Stig Anderson

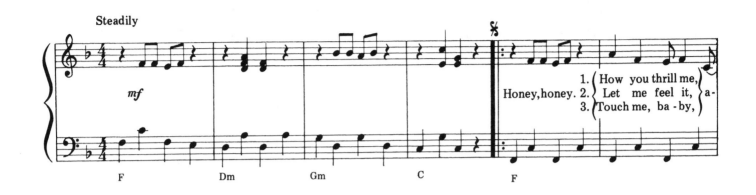

(Oh you make me diz - zy) I don't wan-na hurt you ba-by, I

C   C   Cm7   F7

don't wan-na see you cry.— So stay on the ground girl, You bet-ter not get too high.

Bb   Gm   Cm7   F7

— But I'm gon-na stick to you, boy, You'll

Bb   Fm   Bb7

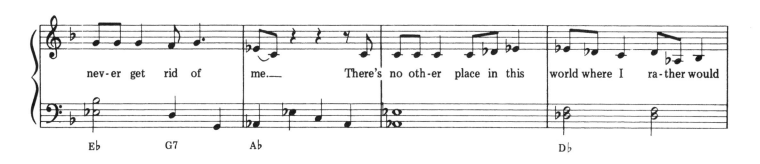

nev-er get rid of me.— There's no oth-er place in this world where I ra-ther would

Eb   G7   Ab   Db

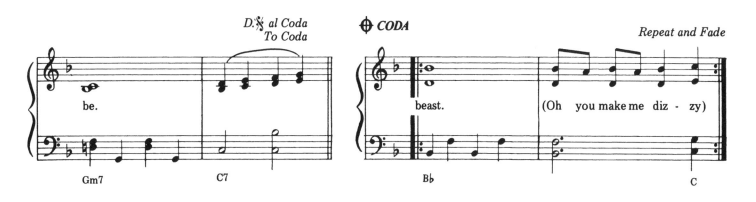

D.%. al Coda
To Coda

⊕ *CODA*

Repeat and Fade

be. beast. (Oh you make me diz - zy)

Gm7   C7   Bb   C

23

I Do, I Do, I Do, I Do, I Do

Words & Music by Benny Andersson, Bjorn Ulvaeus & Stig Anderson

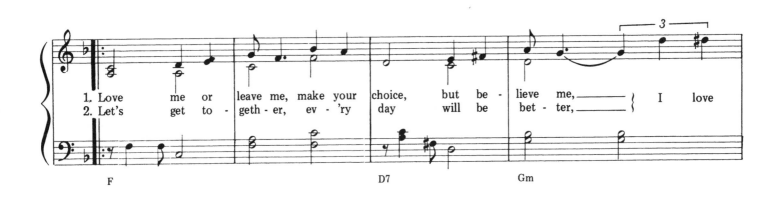

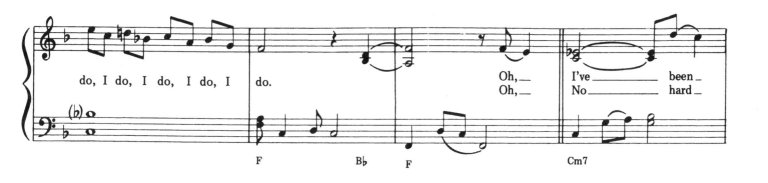

do, I do, I do, I do, I do.   Oh,___ I've_____ been___
Oh,___ No_____ hard___

F   Bb   F   Cm7

dream-in' thru' my   lone - ly___ past.___   Now I just
feel-ings be - tween   you___ and___ me;___   If we can't

F7   Bb   G7

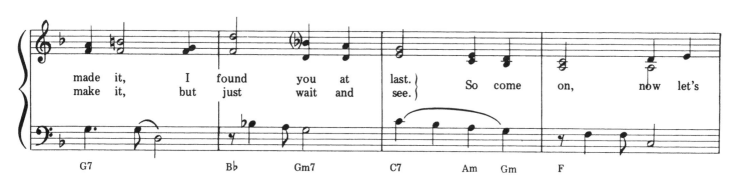

made it,   I found   you at   last.   So come   on,   now let's
make it, but just   you wait and see.

G7   Bb   Gm7   C7   Am Gm   F

try it, I love you, can't de - ny it,___ 'cause it's   true,_____ I

D7   Gm   C7

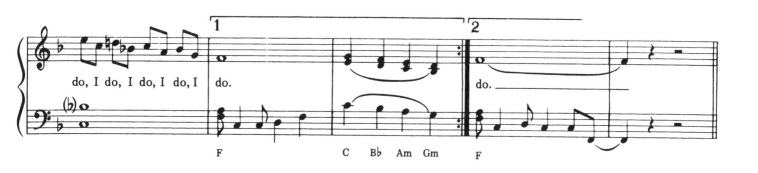

do, I do, I do, I do, I   do.   do.___

F   C Bb Am Gm F

I Have A Dream

Words & Music by Benny Andersson & Bjorn Ulvaeus

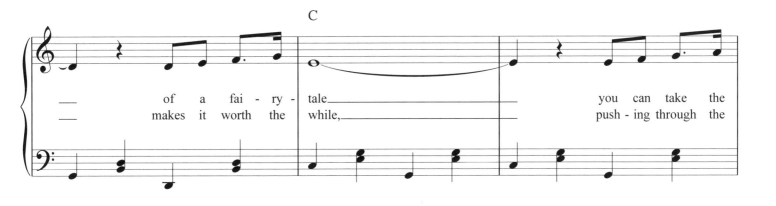

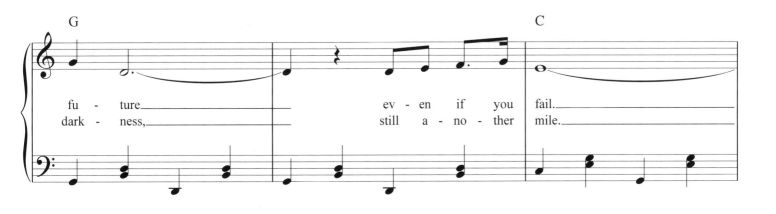

Mamma Mia

Words & Music by Benny Andersson, Bjorn Ulvaeus & Stig Anderson

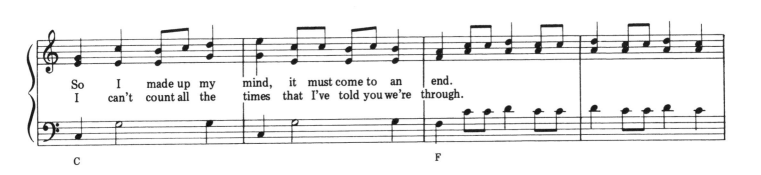

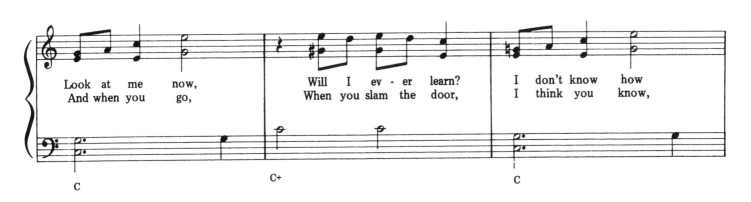

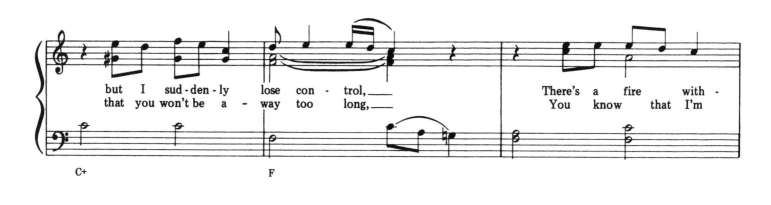

but I sud-den-ly lose con-trol,___
that you won't be a-way too long,___
There's a fire with-
You know that I'm

C+   F

-in my soul.___
not that strong.___
Just a look and I can hear a bell ring, one more

G   F C G   F   C

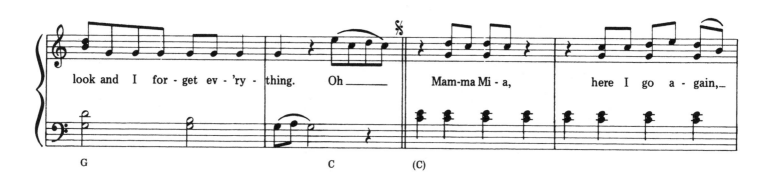

look and I for-get ev-'ry-thing. Oh___ Mam-ma Mi-a, here I go a-gain,___

G   C   (C)

my, my, how can I re-sist you, Mam-ma Mi-a, does it show a-gain.___

Bb   F   C

my, my, just how much I've missed you. Yes___ I've been bro-ken heart-ed,

Bb   F   C   G

blue __ since the day we part-ed. Why, why, did I ev-er let you go, __

Am   Em   B♭   F   Dm7   G7   C

To Coda ⊕

Mam-ma Mi-a, now I real-ly know, __ my, my, I could nev-er let you go. __
(2.) ev-en if I say __

Am7   B♭   F   Dm7   G7   C

bye, bye, leave me now or nev - er; Mam-ma Mi - a, it's a game we play, __

B♭   F   C   Am7

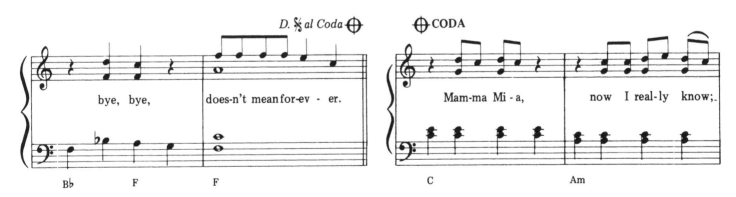

D. % al Coda ⊕   ⊕ CODA

bye, bye, does-n't mean for-ev - er. Mam-ma Mi - a, now I real-ly know; __

B♭   F   F   C   Am

Repeat and Fade

my, my, I could nev-er let you go. __

B♭   F   Dm7   G7   C   C

31

Knowing Me, Knowing You

Words & Music by Benny Andersson, Bjorn Ulvaeus & Stig Anderson

Steady 4

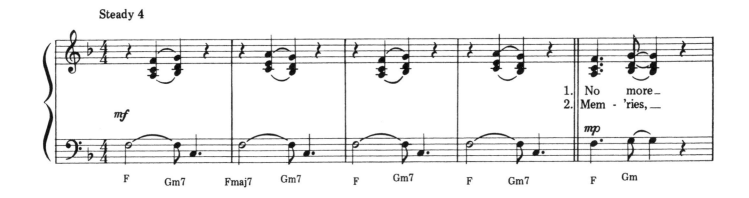

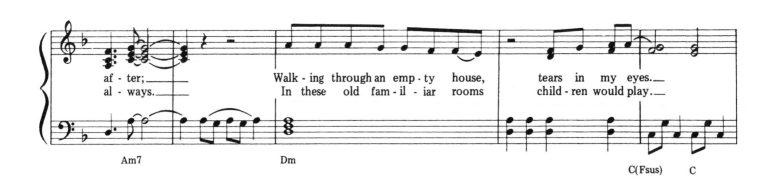

you,　　　　there is no-thing we can　do,　Know-ing me, know-ing you.

C　　　　　　　　　　　　F　　Bb　C

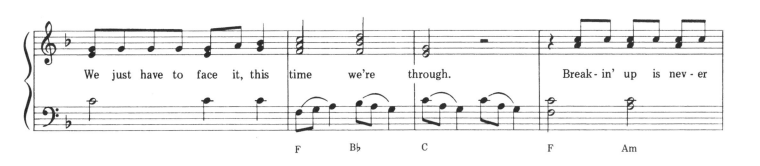

We just have to face it, this time we're through.　Break-in' up is nev-er

F　Bb　C　　　F　Am

To Coda ⊕

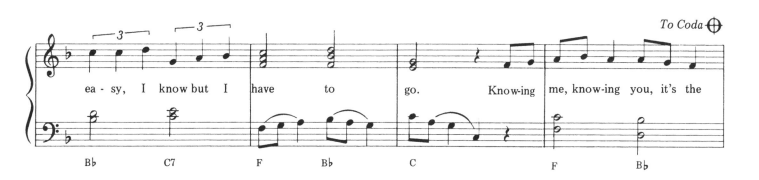

ea-sy, I know but I have　to　go.　Know-ing　me, know-ing you, it's the

Bb　　C7　　F　Bb　C　　　F　Bb

D. %. al Coda ⊕

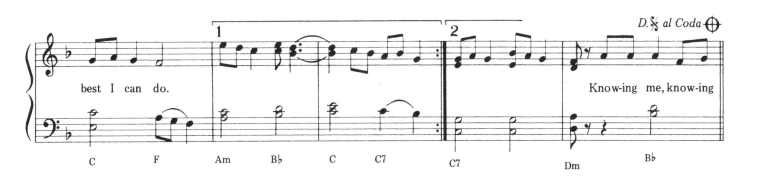

best I can do.　Know-ing me, know-ing

C　F　Am　Bb　C　C7　　C7　　Dm　　Bb

⊕ CODA　　　　　　　　　　　　　　Repeat and Fade

best I can　do.

C　　F　Dm　Am　　Bb　C7

33

Lay All Your Love On Me

Words & Music by Benny Andersson & Bjorn Ulvaeus

now it is-n't true,___ now ev-'ry-thing__ is new__

and all I've learned___ has ov-er-turned,___ I

beg of you:___

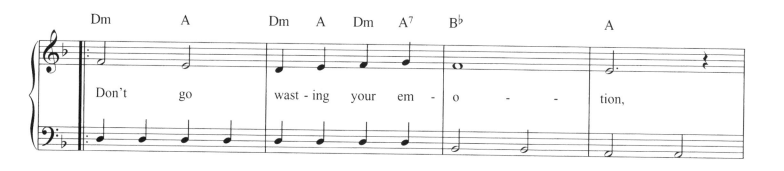

Don't go wast-ing your em-o---tion,

Lay all your love on me.___

1. 2.

Money, Money, Money

Words & Music by Benny Andersson & Bjorn Ulvaeus

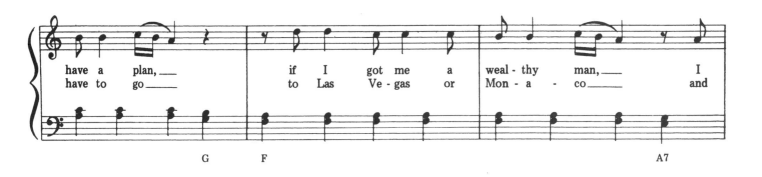

have a plan,____ if I got me a weal-thy man,____ I
have to go____ to Las Ve-gas or Mon-a-co____ and

G   F   A7

ritard.

would-n't have to work at all, I'd fool a-round and have a ball.____
win a for-tune in a game, my life will nev-er be the same.____

Dm   D♯dim

a tempo

Mo-ney, mo-ney, mo-ney

E7   Am E7 Am (Am)

must be fun-ny in the rich man's world.

B7   E7   Am

Mo-ney, mo-ney, mo-ney, al-way's sun-ny in the rich man's

B7   E7

world. A - ha,_____ a - ha.

Am   Dm   E

All the things I could do if I had a lit - tle mo - ney,___

A   Dm   Am   E7   Am

1

it's a rich man's world,

F   E+   Am   F7

it's a rich man's world.   2. A

Dm   E+   Am

2

world.

Am

The Name Of The Game

Words & Music by Benny Andersson, Bjorn Ulvaeus & Stig Anderson

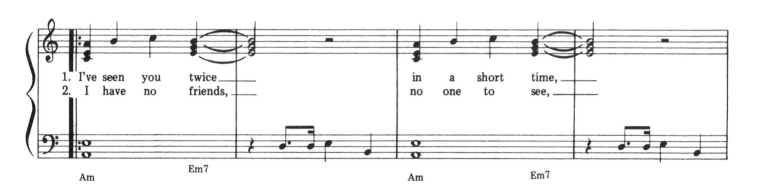

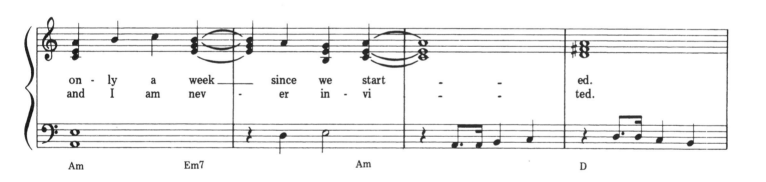

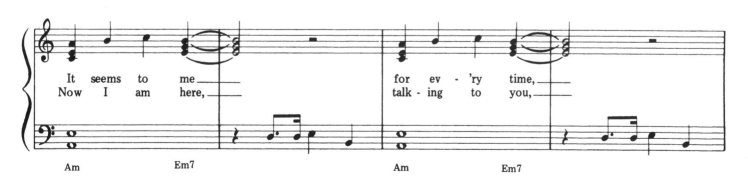

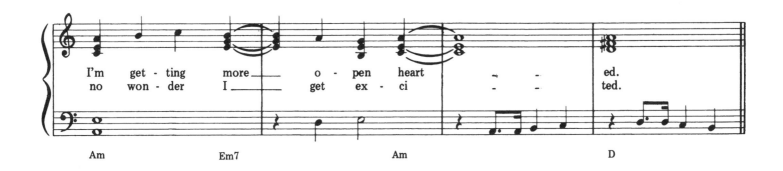

I'm get-ting more___ o - pen heart ___ ed.
no won - der I___ get ex - ci - - - ted.

Am   Em7   Am   D

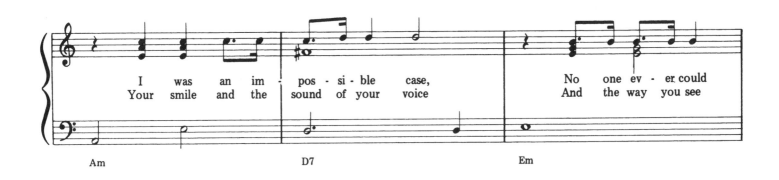

I was an im - pos - si - ble case,   No one ev - er could
Your smile and the sound of your voice   And the way you see

Am   D7   Em

reach___ me,   But I think I can see in your face,
through___ me,   Got - ta feel - ing you gim - me no choice,

F   Am   D7

There's a lot you can teach___ me,___   So I wan - na know. }
But it means a lot to___ me,___   So I wan - na know. }

Em   F

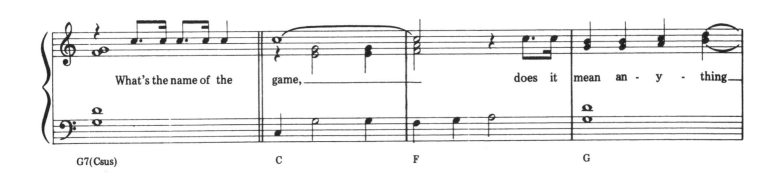

What's the name of the game, ___   does it mean an - y - thing___

G7(Csus)   C   F   G

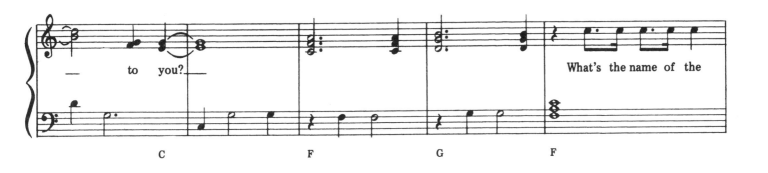

to you? What's the name of the

game, can you feel it the way I do?

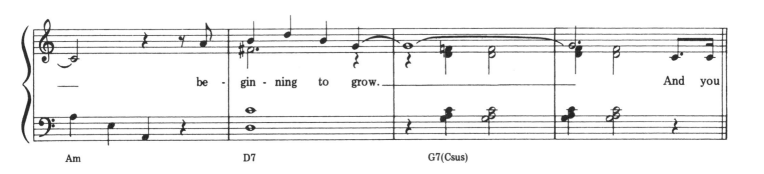

Tell me please 'cause I have to know, I'm a bash-ful child,

be-gin-ning to grow. And you

make me talk, and you make me feel, and you

make me show_____ what I'm try - ing to_____ con - ceal. If I

C   F Bb F C7 F

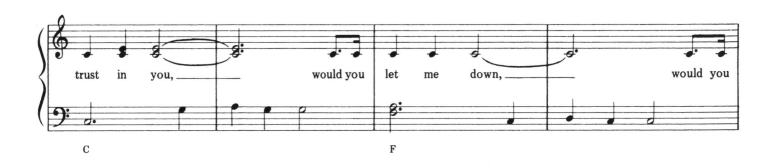

trust in you,_____ would you let me down,_____ would you

C   F

laugh at me?_____ If I said I care_____ for you,

C   Am

Could you feel the same_____ way too? I

Bm7 E   Am

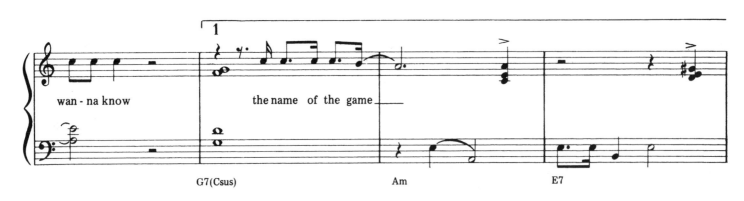

wan - na know   the name of the game_____

G7(Csus)   Am   E7

Am   E7   G7(Csus)

Oh yes I wan - na know

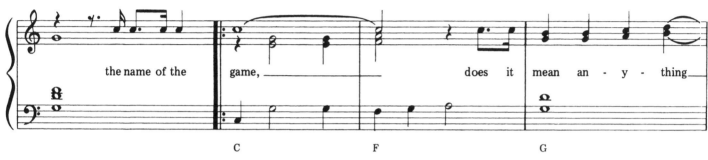

the name of the game, _____ does it mean an - y - thing ____

C   F   G

to you? ____ What's the name of the

C   F   G   F

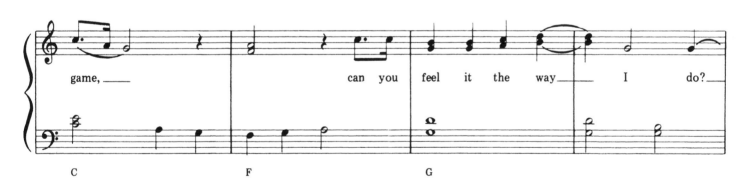

game, ____ can you feel it the way ___ I do? ___

C   F   G

Repeat and Fade

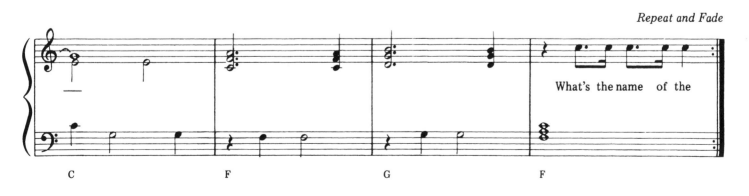

What's the name of the

C   F   G   F

One Of Us

Words & Music by Benny Andersson & Bjorn Ulvaeus

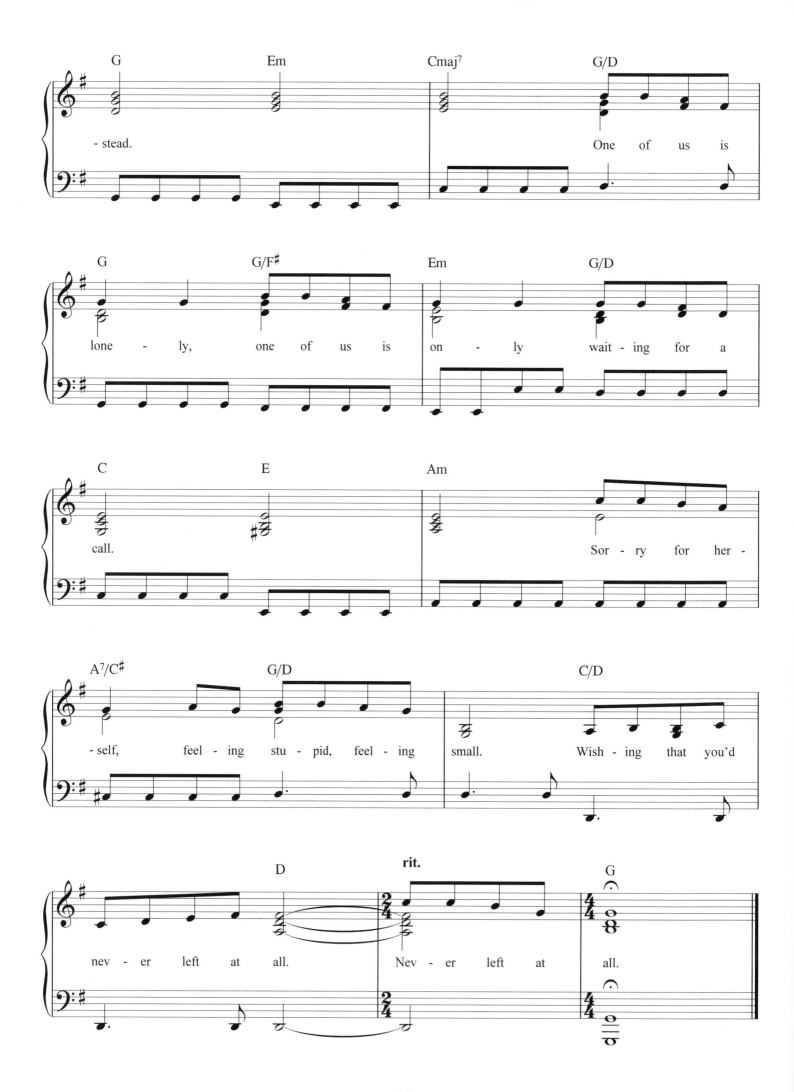

Our Last Summer

Words & Music by Bjorn Ulvaeus & Benny Andersson

S.O.S.

Words & Music by Benny Andersson, Bjorn Ulvaeus & Stig Anderson

Super Trouper

Words & Music by Benny Andersson & Bjorn Ulvaeus

1. I was sick and tired of ev - 'ry - thing_____ when I called_____ you last night from
2. Fac - ing twen - ty thou - sand of your friends,_____ how can a - ny - one be so

Glas - gow.   All I do is eat and sleep and sing,_____ wish - ing ev -
lone - ly?   Part of a suc - cess that nev - er ends,_____ still I'm think -

57

Slipping Through My Fingers

Words & Music by Benny Andersson & Bjorn Ulvaeus

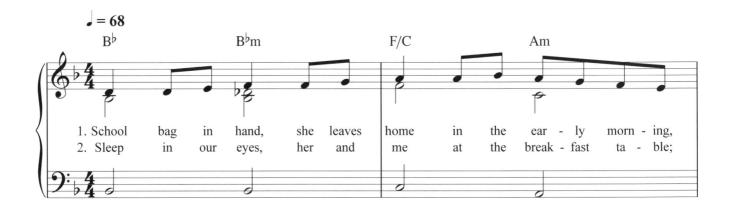

1. School bag in hand, she leaves home in the ear-ly morn-ing,
2. Sleep in our eyes, her and me at the break-fast ta-ble;

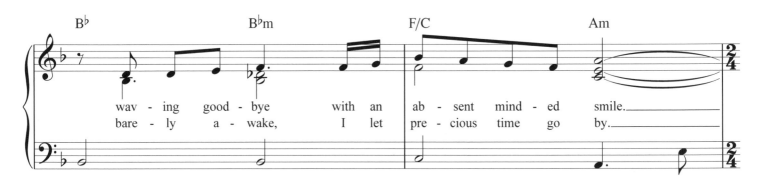

wav-ing good-bye with an ab-sent mind-ed smile.
bare-ly a-wake, I let pre-cious time go by.

— I watch her go with a surge of that well known sad-ness
— Then when she's gone there's that old me-lan-cho-ly feel-ing

and I have to sit down for a while. The
and a sense of guilt I can't de-ny. What

fing - ers all the time. Do I real - ly see what's in her mind? Each time I

think I'm close to know -ing_____ she keeps on grow - ing. Slip-ping through my

1.

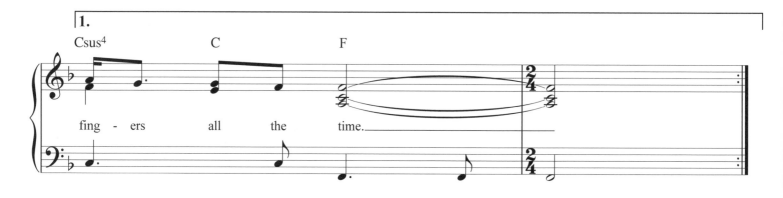

fing - ers all the time._____

2.

fing - ers all the time._____ Some - times I wish that I could freeze the

pic - ture_____ and save it from the fun - ny tricks of

time, slip - ping through my fing - ers.___

Instrumental

School bag in hand, she leaves home in the ear - ly morn - ing,

wav - ing good - bye with an ab - sent mind - ed smile.

Thank You For The Music

Words & Music by Benny Andersson & Bjorn Ulvaeus

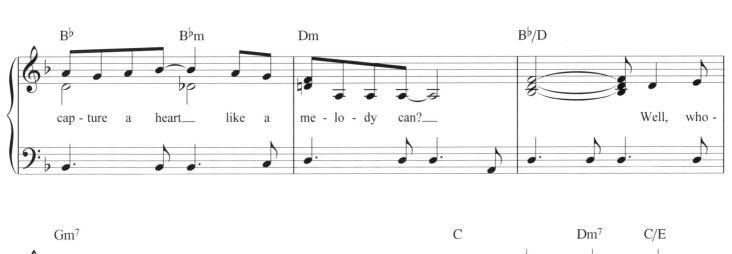

B♭   B♭m   Dm   B♭/D

cap - ture a heart___ like a me - lo - dy can?___ Well, who -

Gm⁷   C   Dm⁷   C/E

-ev - er it was,_____ I'm a fan.___ So I say

F   Gm⁷   C   F

thank you for the mu - sic, the songs I'm sing - ing.

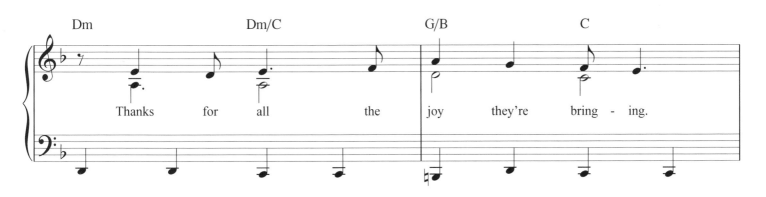

Dm   Dm/C   G/B   C

Thanks for all the joy they're bring - ing.

F   Gm⁷   A   Dm

Who can live with - out it? I ask in all ho - nes - ty___

I wan-na sing__ it out__ to ev - 'ry - bo - dy.

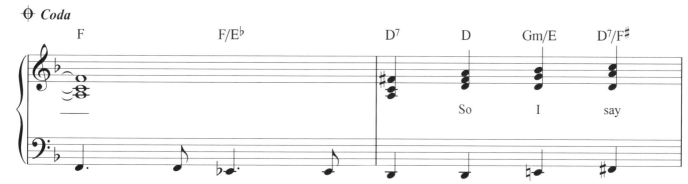

rit.

What a joy,____ what a life,_____ what a chance.__

D.S. al Coda

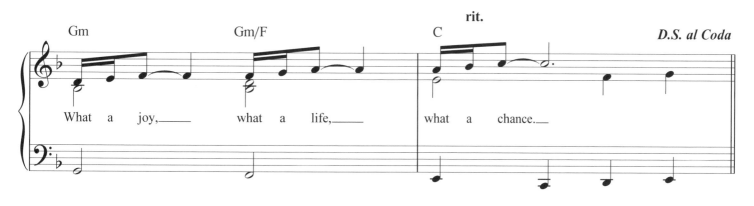

Coda

So I say

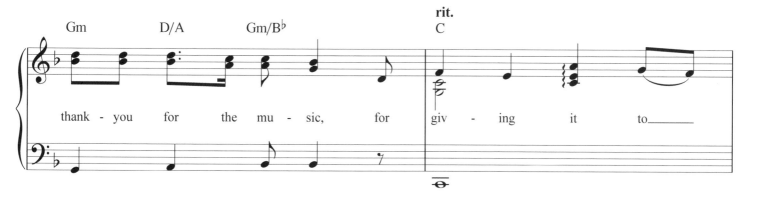

rit.

thank - you for the mu - sic, for giv - ing it to_____

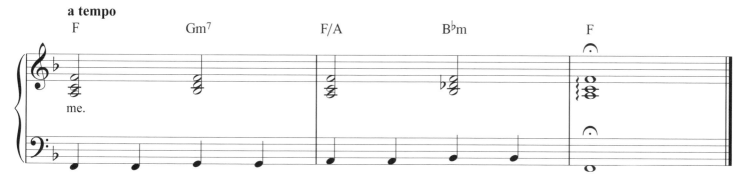

a tempo

me.

Take A Chance On Me

Words & Music by Benny Andersson & Bjorn Ulvaeus

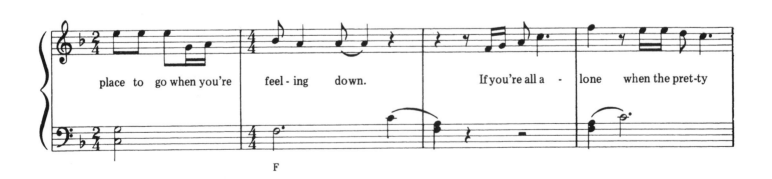

birds have flown, Ho-ney, I'm still free, take a chance on me. gon-na do my

C7

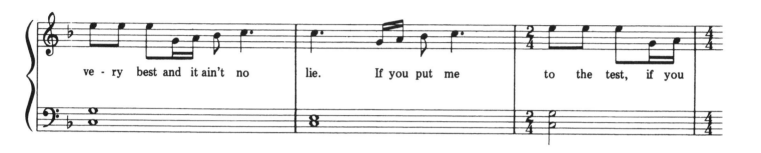

ve - ry best and it ain't no lie. If you put me to the test, if you

let me try, __ Take a chance on me, __ take a chance on me. __

F Gm C7 Gm

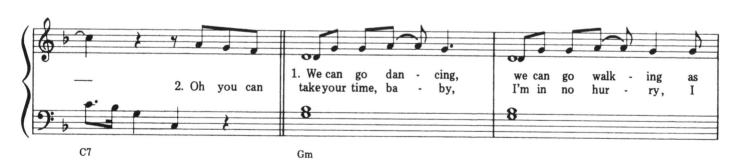

2. Oh you can

1. We can go dan - cing, take your time, ba - by, we can go walk - ing as I'm in no hur - ry, I

C7 Gm

long as we're to - geth - er;
know I'm gon - na get you;

lis - ten to some mu - sic,
you don't wan - na hurt me,

F Gm

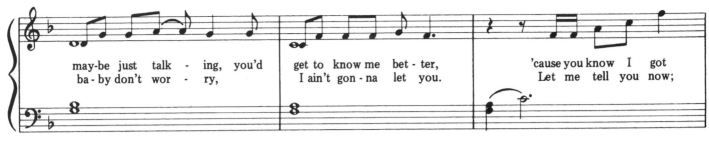

may-be just talk - ing, you'd
ba - by don't wor - ry,

get to know me bet - ter,
I ain't gon - na let you.

'cause you know I got
Let me tell you now;

F

so much that I wan - na do.
my love is strong e - nough

When I dream I'm a - lone with you, it's
to__ last when things are rough, it's

ma - gic.__
ma - gic.__

Dm   Bb   Dm   Bb   C

You want me to leave it there,
You say that I waste my time,

a - fraid of a love af - fair, but I
but I can't get it off my mind, No I

think you know__
can't let go,__

Dm   Bb   Gm

that I can't let go.__
'cause I love you so.__

1
If you change your

2
(me)   If you change your

C7   Gm   C   F   F

Repeat and Fade

mind,   I'm the first in   line,   Ho-ney I'm still   free,   take a chance on

C7

68

Under Attack

Words & Music by Benny Andersson & Bjorn Ulvaeus

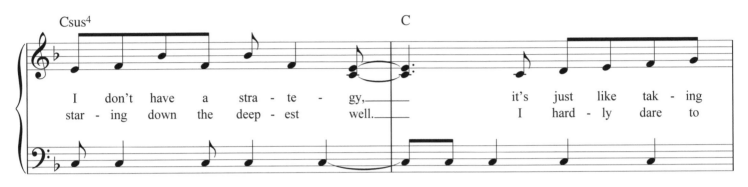

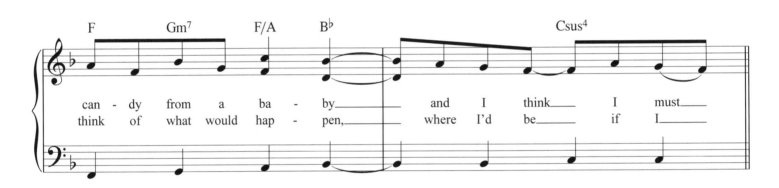

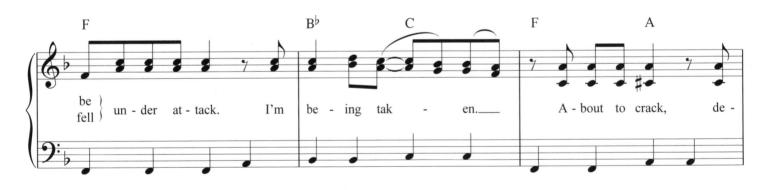

Voulez-Vous

Words & Music by Benny Andersson & Bjorn Ulvaeus

73

The Winner Takes It All

Words & Music by Benny Andersson & Bjorn Ulvaeus

77

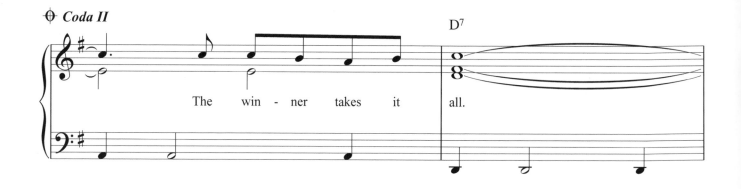

The win - ner takes it all.

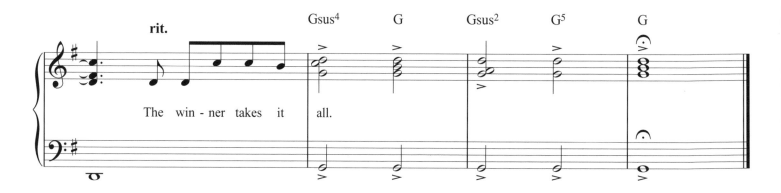

The win - ner takes it all.

Verse 3:
Tell me does she kiss
Like I used to kiss you?
Does it feel the same
When she calls your name?
Somewhere deep inside
You must know I miss you
But what can I say
Rules must be obeyed.

The judges will decide
The likes of me abide
Spectators of the show
Always staying low.

Verse 4:
I don't wanna talk
'Cause it makes me feel sad
And I understand
You've come to shake my hand
I apologise
If it makes you feel bad
Seeing me so tense
No self-confidence
But you see
The winner takes it all
The winner takes it all.

3456789
9/08 (167031)